Broadband Talent Management:
Paths to Improvement

Robert W. Eichinger
Michael M. Lombardo
Alex Stiber

Broadband Talent Management:
Paths to Improvement

Robert W. Eichinger
Michael M. Lombardo
Alex Stiber

Published by Lominger International: A Korn/Ferry Company
Minneapolis, Minnesota 55416-2291
Tel. 952-345-3600 • Fax. 952-345-3601 • www.lominger.com

FYI For Your Improvement™ is the exclusive trademark of
Lominger International: A Korn/Ferry Company

Printed in the United States of America
by TM Associates, Inc.
Cover Design: Lodermeier Montei Design

ISBN: 0-9745892-9-2
Lominger reorder part number: 11033

FIRST EDITION MAY 2005
SECOND PRINTING JUNE 2005
THIRD PRINTING MARCH 2006
FOURTH PRINTING NOVEMBER 2007
REPRINT JANUARY 2010

About the Authors

Mike Lombardo has over 30 years experience in executive and management research and in executive coaching and training. He has worked with hundreds of corporations in the US and Europe. He is one of the founders of Lominger Limited, Inc., (now Lominger International: A Korn/Ferry Company) publishers of The LEADERSHIP ARCHITECT® Suite. With Bob Eichinger, Mike has authored 40 products for the suite, including *The Leadership Machine, FYI For Your Improvement*™, *100 Things You Need to Know*, The CAREER ARCHITECT®, CHOICES ARCHITECT®, and VOICES®, the first electronic 360-degree instrument. The LEADERSHIP ARCHITECT® suite contains products that deal with employee development, interviewing for selection, succession planning, feedback, learning skills, performance management, culture assessment, and team building.

During his 15 years at the Center for Creative Leadership, Mike was a co-author of *The Lessons of Experience*, which detailed the experiences that can teach the competencies needed to be successful. He also co-authored the research on executive derailment revealing how personal flaws and overdone strengths caused otherwise effective executives to get into career trouble, BENCHMARKS®, one of the first 360-degree feedback instruments, and the LOOKING GLASS® simulation, a simulation of managerial work that is used internationally. With Bob Eichinger, he developed the popular program, "Tools for Developing Successful Executives," an international offering of the Center for Creative Leadership.

He has won four national awards for research on managerial and executive development. He has co-authored or edited seven books and over 50 publications in popular and professional journals.

Bob Eichinger is CEO of Lominger International: A Korn/Ferry Company and, along with Mike Lombardo, co-creator of The LEADERSHIP ARCHITECT® Suite of manager and executive development products and co-author of *The Leadership Machine*, a source book on developing people. Bob has over 40 years experience in management and executive development. He held executive development positions at PepsiCo and Pillsbury and has consulted with hundreds of organizations on succession planning and development. He has lectured extensively on the topic of executive and management development and has served on the Board of the Human Resource Planning Society, a professional association of people charged with the responsibility of management and executive development in their organizations. He has been a one-on-one feedback giver and coach from both inside and outside organizations. Bob has worked personally with over 1,000 managers and executives during his career. He has served on feedback teams within courses and off-sites in various organizations and public courses.

Alex Stiber is an author and consultant who has worked extensively in the area of organizational culture change. He's designed and implemented training and development programs and facilitated change initiatives for many *Fortune 500* organizations.

Acknowledgements

The authors are, as always, grateful to many people for their input, ideas, and contributions.

We would like, in particular, to thank Lesley Kurke, especially for action orientation, priority setting, planning, patience, time management, and written communications—just a few of her many strengths.

To Cara Capretta Raymond, thanks for the insight, motivation, perspective, and creativity.

To Lominger Associates, and especially Linda Hodge and Linda Rodman, who have, despite their demanding schedules, given us all the feedback we could hope for (and then some)—our appreciation.

We are truly impressed with the ownership so many people were eager to take regarding this work, with or without formal acknowledgement.

There are more things in heaven and earth, Horatio,
Than are dreamt of in your philosophy.

Hamlet, by William Shakespeare

TABLE OF CONTENTS

TABLE OF CONTENTS

INTRODUCTION

You've received 360-degree feedback. And you've had your performance appraisal. They have both confirmed what you most likely already know and what everyone else who knows you knows: You're imperfect. (If you think you *are* perfect, have we got a plan for you!)

That's not to say you aren't doing a good job. Or maybe even a great job. What it is saying is that if you were to address some areas (for the sake of our discussion, let's call them competencies) related to how you get your job done, your overall performance would improve.

Ah, but you've probably received this feedback before. Remember your last 360-degree feedback report? At the end it provided you with developmental suggestions on what to do about your three lowest-rated competencies, offered some tips on how to behave, workshops to look for, job activities that might stretch you, and books to read…. And you cherry-picked from those lists and pasted stuff into the development-planning template. Then you and your boss reviewed it and signed it. And guess what: A year later, not much had changed.

Why? Didn't you follow the plan?

Sure you did. You targeted what your report told you were your three weakest areas (sometimes referred to, euphemistically, as "your three greatest development opportunities") and then did what the development plan told you to do. And yet nothing much changed.

Did you fail to "fix what's wrong"?

Maybe yes, maybe no.

Does it make a difference?

Again, maybe yes, maybe no.

The insights we're getting from research (e.g., Baldwin & Padgett, 1993; McCall et al., 1988) and experience tell us that one of the basic problems with the conventionally accepted approach to "developmental planning" around performance and 360-degree feedback is rooted in the notion that all you need to do is identify what's "wrong" and then fix it. Clean and simple.

Except that it's not. When you look at the ways in which people improve their performance, you find that there are far more *strategies* and *tactics* (in everyday language, "ways" or "paths") by which people manage to improve their *outcomes*. And most of us would agree that in organizations, outcomes are fundamentally more important than activities (assuming, of course, that the activities involved in achieving outcomes aren't detrimental to other aspects of organizational functioning and to other people).

Consider, for example, the difference in potential impact between asking someone, "What are you doing?" and "What are you accomplishing?"

The limitation of conventional approaches to "development plans" is that they are, in general, focused on activities rather than outcomes. They tell you to do this, then do that, then do something else, and, *voila*, you'll get better ratings next time you participate in the 360-degree feedback program.

The 360-degree feedback report says, "Hi, Pat Sample. Here are your problem areas ('developmental opportunities')," and the development plan says, "I've got your answer…right here." Nowhere does the plan engage you in a process of understanding what underlies these areas of relative need. That is, the conventional approaches and the prefab plans don't help you to *know* yourself.

The assumption that every weakness should be strengthened and everything that's broken can be fixed is simply wrong. That doesn't mean you have license to simply ignore it all. Quite the opposite. What you do have license to do, however, is approach those needs from a variety of perspectives, all of which are equally legitimate, as we'll see.

So, what's the status of typical development plans?

◆ In spite of efforts to improve them, development plans are mostly pathetic.

A major player in the medical device industry conducted an audit of the development plans they had in place for all of their executives. The purpose of the audit was to determine if there was a general pattern to the developmental needs of their executive population. Astonishingly, 82% of the development plans suggested the executive take a course. Notwithstanding at least 80 research studies showing that a good development plan should emphasize "experiences," taking a course was the developmental remedy of overwhelming choice.

◆ Development plans, if they are created, are not implemented.

During the course of a 360-degree feedback session, a senior executive stated that he has known about his developmental need for a number of years. In fact, he has had the same development plan for five years: to take a course on strategic planning at a leading university. Unfortunately, every year that he signed up for the course something interfered—business demands, personal demands—and besides, he had been promoted and didn't think it was important any longer. Somewhat prophetically, he was going through the 360-degree feedback process because he was derailing in his current position, in which strategic agility was crucial for his success.

BACKGROUND

Research (Lombardo & Eichinger, 2004; Goleman, 1998; Boyatzis, 1982) has shown that managers, leaders, and individual contributors who know themselves better are more successful than those who don't. They know themselves better in part because they are more likely to seek feedback in many forms, quicker to accept it, and more likely to act on it.

How they act on it—how they *respond*—is a topic we've been most interested in learning more about. And what we have learned is that there are many more ways than the conventional development plan approach by which one may successfully act on an identified need.

Recent research (e.g., Zenger & Folkman, 2002; Lombardo, 2004) tells us that successful managers achieve their success based on a handful of (about four to seven) key strengths. That's not to say that every successful executive focuses on the same four to seven areas. In fact, there are eighteen strengths that collectively differentiate the super successful from the unsuccessful. But, within those eighteen, the research shows that you can have any four to seven in the upper 15% of your ratings compared to others and be successful.

Does that mean all you need to be concerned about are a few key strengths? Surely there must be more to it. And there is. Research (Lombardo & Eichinger, 2004) shows not only do you need that handful of mission-critical strengths, but also two more things are important. First, those mission-critical competencies which are not strengths must not be generating any "noise"—that is, while you don't rely on them to provide the platform for stellar performance, they're not getting in the way; they're not distracting; they're neutralized. And second, you can have no fatal flaws.

So, given that you have a sufficient number of strengths in mission-critical areas, and that you are not only open to feedback but seek it and proactively address areas of need, what ways other than the conventional development plan are there for you to address those needs? What are the options—within the context of what we'll refer to as *Broadband Talent Management*—for responding?

By the way, in case you're thinking, "But I heard you only need to focus on your strengths and find the right place for yourself," here's what research shows may happen if you heed that advice:

- ◆ Strengths have a career half-life. Seven strengths in a forty-five-year career put you, at forty-something, in grave danger of derailing.

- ◆ Overuse moves a strength to the dark side.

- ◆ Your flaws catch up with you.

- ◆ Of all feedback forms, self-assessment is the least accurate. (And lack of self-awareness of what you overuse is the big derailer.)

Some of what matters for an executive doesn't matter until you get there—then overuses hit like a truck.

Who Is This Broadband System For?

The Broadband Talent Management options are for individuals seeking alternatives for improving their performance and potential, and it is for coaches, mentors, bosses, or HR professionals—that is, anyone who is helping others with improvement or personal effectiveness.

But not everyone has access to a coach. For those who don't, think of this book as your coach: When you see yourself in one of the cases or descriptions of commonly observed responses to feedback, see if one of the plans described here might be a good fit to your need.

Broadband Talent Management: The Plans

So far, we've found that there are 16 paths to improvement—16 types of plans to follow up on feedback:

As you look over this list, you may wonder if we're splitting hairs here and there. And to that charge we'll plead guilty. But *the sometimes subtle differences are important* because they point to different actions: Each plan derives either from a context that is unique, or points to a unique set of actions.

QUICK START

Before we cover each Path or Plan in detail, here is a short form to get you started:

1. **Development Plan**—A plan designed to work directly on a need, weakness, or developmental opportunity on a mission-critical competency or a competency that's getting in the way of performing or furthering a career; the person is aware and agrees and is motivated to do something about it; the remedy is a typical IDP (Individual Development Plan) created against the 70jobs/20people/10courses finding on how to build competencies; the plan is created by the individual, a boss, coach or mentor, or a development facilitator, signed off on by the boss and the organization and tracked for effectiveness; the goal is to get a weakness out of the noise zone into average or neutral; the skill needed to create such a plan is moderate, and the resources for the content of such a plan are abundant.

2. **Enhancement Plan**—A plan designed to work on an average skill or competency that's on the mission-critical list or one that would greatly help this person perform better; based on feedback that the person is at the fully-meets-expectations level; person is aware, agrees the skill is average and is motivated to improve it; the remedy is a 70/20/10 IDP created by the individual, boss, coach, mentor, or development facilitator, signed off on by the boss and the organization, and tracked for effectiveness; the goal is to move the skill from average to a strength; the skill needed to create such a plan is expert, and the resources for the content of such a plan are abundant; this plan is generally easier than working on something that is low or a weakness.

3. **Good to Great Plan**—A plan designed to take a strength and make it great or outstanding (upper 10% of people at the same level); the person is aware, agrees and is motivated to work on a strength to make it even better (brings to mind the fact that Tiger Woods still takes lessons!); the remedy is a plan put together by a skills coach who knows what top performance looks like and how to get there; the plan would have to be created by an expert in this competency, agreed to by the individual, the boss, and the organization, and tracked for effectiveness; the goal is to take something the person is already very good at and make him/her great; the skills needed to create such a plan are specialized, and there are but a few able to do it for each competency; resources for such a plan are scarce, with a lot coming from the personal experience of an expert skills coach.

4. **Workaround Plan**—A plan designed to achieve an outcome the person is struggling with because of a lack of skill or a low-rated competency; accomplished by using other resources instead of building the missing skill; the person is aware, agrees and wants to do something about it; the plan might include using other people who are good at the missing skill, changing the nature of the task, changing the nature of the job to de-emphasize the area of struggle, or by redefining self; the person is motivated to produce the outcome but not by fixing the missing skill; the remedy is to find some other way to get the same thing done without having

to work on building the missing skill directly; the boss and the organization need to be informed that this approach was selected over a direct Development Plan and agree to the path because some may think of this as avoidance of the issue; the plan could be created by the individual, the boss, coach, mentor, or development facilitator; the content of the plan is available, and the skill to create the plan is moderate.

(**NOTE:** A Workaround Plan involves using a resource other than self, whereas a Substitution Plan involves only the person.)

5. **Substitution Plan**—A plan designed to accomplish an outcome the person is struggling with because of a lack of skill or a low-rated competency; accomplished by upgrading the use of other skills and competencies he or she has at the average or above-average level; the plan does not include working on the missing skill directly; the person is aware, agrees and is motivated to do something about it; the remedy is to find other skills, talents, experiences, and competencies the person already has that can act like or cover for the missing skill; the boss and the organization need to know that this path is being used in lieu of a direct Development Plan and agree to the plan because some may see this as avoiding the real issue; the plan could be created by a coach or a development facilitator; the content of the plan is available, but the skill needed to create such a plan is at the moderate to expert level.

(**NOTE:** A Substitution Plan involves only the person, whereas a Workaround Plan involves using a resource other than self.)

6. **Redeployment Plan**—A plan designed for the person and the organization to make better use of the portfolio of strengths and average skills; the person is aware, understands, agrees to the plan, and is motivated to get to a better place; the remedy is to find another job, role, unit, or even company where the skills fit in better; there is no effort to improve; the individual, boss, and the organization need to understand that a Redeployment path is being selected in lieu of a direct Development Plan because some would see this as avoiding the issue; the plan includes helping the person understand what the negative consequences might be of not working on any personal improvement; the plan needs to be created by a coach or development facilitator knowledgeable about where this person's skills might better fit; the skill needed to do this is minimal and the methods and resources are readily available.

7. **Capitulation Plan**—Less a plan, more of a life or career choice, being unmotivated, or just giving up; the choice is to do nothing about any weaknesses or developmental opportunities in mission-critical areas or any other area that's causing noise; the person is aware of the issues, agrees to them but is not motivated to do anything about them; the "plan" is to help the person to understand the possible consequences of inaction; the consequences might include being removed from a job that's needed for another more ambitious individual, a lesser more-focused role, or even separation from the company; the boss and the organization need to be informed of the choice to not do anything to improve as this will be seen as avoiding the issue; the choice can be managed by a very knowledgeable boss, coach, mentor,

or development facilitator; the skills needed to create this plan are minimal and involve knowing what the real consequences might be.

8. **Compensation Plan**—A plan designed to neutralize the noise caused by the overuse of a strength by using other skills that have a dampening effect on the noise; it's a version of the Substitution Plan, but the subtle difference is that auxiliary skills are used to quell the noise, not accomplish what the overused skill does; overused skills cause collateral damage to other people and to the organization; the person understands the problem and is motivated to do something about it, but most people will rightly resist anything that suggests doing less of a strength; the plan depends upon the person having one or more noise-chilling skills—if he/she doesn't, then the plan would shift to a direct Development or Enhancement Plan to build some; the plan can be created by a coach or development facilitator; the coaching skills needed are moderate and involve knowing what skills cover for what overused skills; the resources are readily available; the goal is to have the person continue to apply the strength, even to excess, but to cover the negative consequences with lubricating or noise-canceling skills.

9. **Rerailment Plan**—A plan designed to help a person who has fallen off the career track because of one or more severe stumbles; generally due to the existence of one or more significant derailers or career stallers and stoppers; the person is aware of the problems that have led to the derailment, agrees to them and is highly motivated to get back on track; the plan involves identifying the derailers or stallers that have caused the problem and working to address them; the work includes decreasing the derailers by a combination of self-awareness and coaching; Workarounds and Substitutes are also possibilities as well as a direct Development Plan; the plan requires a coach or a development facilitator to create and execute; the resources are available but complex; the goal is to assure that the derailers are neutralized and will not again lead to trouble, and that the remaining skills are enough to allow the person to continue performing and have a satisfying career.

10. **Marketing Plan**—A plan designed to persuade observers that the person really does have the skill they don't think he or she has; the person is aware that the perception gap exists and is motivated to correct it; the boss, coach, mentor, or development facilitator are also aware of the gap, believe the person really is skilled, and believe closing the gap will be useful; the plan involves creating a Marketing Plan to offer proof, examples, demonstrations, and other evidence that the person is really skilled in an area; usually the skill in question is an important one, otherwise it wouldn't be a problem; this situation occurs when the person's background is not well known to the raters, or the current job doesn't offer much opportunity to exhibit the skill; the plan can be created by the individual, boss, coach, mentor, or development facilitator; the goal is to correct a perception gap observers have that, if not corrected, might lead to some negative consequences when rewards or promotions are decided upon.

11. **Skills Transfer Plan**—A plan designed to help a person transfer skills used in one context or situation to another (usually work); the person is aware that he or she is skilled in the area in question in some settings but not in others, agrees to it and is motivated to transfer those skills to another setting; the plan involves examining the effective behaviors being applied in one setting, finding their equivalents in another, and planning for the transfer; a Skills Transfer Plan, although rarer, is cheaper and faster than a Development Plan; an insightful boss, coach, mentor, or development facilitator can create the plan; the skills involved to create the plan are minimal and include knowing what has blocked the skills transfer thus far and techniques for transfer of skills; the goal is to help the person transfer an existing skill to a new setting.

12. **Exposure Plan**—A plan designed to get an initial estimate of how skilled a person is in an area where there has been no opportunity to perform; we usually refer to this as an "untested" area; observers either answer "don't know" when asked, which is preferred, or unfortunately might indicate a lower rating or evaluation; the person also doesn't know skill level and considers this an untested area; he or she is motivated to find out; usually the skill is an important one or it wouldn't be an issue; the plan involves finding viable opportunities for the person to try out the skill or competency; the recommendation is to start small and work up to more significant challenges; the best bet is that the person is below average or low because they have never done this before in any significant setting; the plan can be created by the individual, the boss, coach or mentor, or a development facilitator; the skills required to create the plan are moderate; the goal is to discover the starting point for the skill; once known, if it turns out to be a problem, then other plans apply.

13. **Confidence Building Plan**—A plan designed to increase the ego, self-esteem, confidence, and self-deployment of a person who is significantly more skilled than he or she knows or is willing to admit; there are two versions of this plan: there is one for people who really don't know how good they are or could be—the plan in that case assists in offering calibration proof of where the person stands in relation to others; the other cause is unjustified humility, where the person doesn't feel right about taking personal credit for accomplishments—in that case the plan is more one of counseling and mentoring; the person is probably not really aware, and underestimates skills and accomplishments to a significant degree; the two plans are somewhat different in terms of the skills needed to create the plans; in the case of the person just not knowing, creating the calibration proof is needed; in the case of the person knowing but not feeling good about acknowledging it, the skill involved is really a form of counseling; the latter requires more skill; the goal is to increase the accuracy of self-knowledge thereby increasing self-confidence and self-deployment.

14. **Insight Plan**—A plan designed to help a person gain deeper insight into overrated skills and competencies; usually called blind spots, these are areas others rate as low and the person rates as high; there are two versions of this plan: in one version, it is a true blind spot; the person actually thinks he or she is much better than

everyone around them thinks; the remedy in that version is to offer additional proof the person would more likely believe; the proof can be from other respected sources, mentors, past bosses, or it can be more formal assessment; the other version involves a person who actually does know how bad he or she is but refuses to acknowledge it or rate in line with his/her true view; the skills needed to create a plan for this situation are significant because you are dealing with a defensive person in a negative process; dealing effectively in this case usually requires a skilled coach or development facilitator and might involve the help of a mentor or trusted associate; the goal is to get the person to become more accurately aware of issues; once that is achieved, some of the other plans will apply.

15. **Diagnostic Plan**—A plan designed to collect additional information about a confusing pattern of ratings and evaluations; this occurs when either different groups or constituencies rate the person significantly different or when even within the same group the evaluations of the same skill range widely; the person may or may not be in touch with the results, may or may not agree with them, and may or may not know why the results are as they are; the plan involves digging more deeply into the confusing results to find out the why behind the discrepancies; it may involve additional data collection and involve other knowledgeable and trusted sources; in the case of a cooperative and knowledgeable person, the task to create such a plan is straightforward although it may be complex; in the case of a defensive person lacking self-awareness, the task to create this plan is difficult; the inquiry is into why different groups and/or different people see this person differently on the same skills and competencies; more often than not, the answer lies in the person's psyche and background, and a personality assessment is a useful addition to this; this plan can be created by a coach or development facilitator; the goal is to bring the person to awareness of the cause or causes of the differential ratings or evaluations; once that is achieved, some of the other plans apply.

16. **Assessment Plan**—A plan designed to discover a deeper and underlying problem that is affecting performance or general behavior; this is usually a personal or interpersonal problem that is of more recent origin that is causing a lot of noise in the workplace; the person may or may not be aware of the underlying problem or the trouble it's causing; many times he or she is not able to perform as in the past and is acting out frustrations by exhibiting disruptive behaviors; in the case of a person who understands there is a problem and wants to address it, the remedy involves engaging professional help; in the case of a person who is generally not aware of what's going on, the remedy is much more complex and may require moving to an Insight Plan first and then returning to this plan; the coaching skills required to manage this kind of situation are in the expert class; only very skilled coaches and development facilitators are trained to be helpful in these cases; the goal is to identify the underlying problem and then design a treatment plan; once the underlying problem is successfully addressed, the person can return to his or her previous portfolio of strengths.

Now we will cover each of the plans in more depth.

Development Plan

///

1. Development Plan: Working on a weakness

This plan, sometimes called an Individual Development Plan, or IDP, is the ubiquitous plan we've all used. When you adopt this plan, you're deciding that you're going to *fix* one or more weaknesses. (Remember: Superior performers have no weaknesses—no noise—in the mission-critical areas.)

When we talk about "fixing" a weakness, we're not suggesting that your goal should be to move it from a weakness to a strength (arguably an unrealistic goal), but rather to reduce the noise, move it to a level of acceptable performance. For example, let's say your job requires you to listen to others, and your 360-degree feedback says you don't do that particularly well. You know from experience that they're right—you do have a hard time listening without interrupting and finishing other people's statements, and you're often thinking about what you're going to say next while someone else is talking. In fact, you are aware enough of it that you have occasionally wished there was a switch on the back of your head that you could toggle when you need to be quiet and listen. Only thing is, sometimes you're also impatient, and so you may not think to flip the switch even if you could. (Can you imagine that some people might perceive you to be arrogant?)

The good news is, it's not hopeless. You are more prone to humility than perhaps others know: You listen well enough to have heard the feedback, you've accepted it, and now you're determined to do something about it. But what?

If we're to believe what the research from the Center for Creative Leadership tells us (e.g., McCall, Lombardo, & Morrison, 1988; Morrison, White, & VanVelsor, 1987, rev. 1992), we know several things about developing a skill.

◆ *See the target.* We understand that if we're going to develop a skill, we first need to know what the target looks like. So, you think of someone who is widely considered to be a good listener. You picture that person listening in meetings. You note the things that person does—the body language and the verbal responses. You develop a model of the effective listener and establish that as your reference standard.

◆ *See yourself in comparison to the target.* Then compare yourself to that person. What is the distance between you and your model? What does he or she do that you don't do? If you aren't sure, whom could you ask? And how would asking (for feedback) be aligned with your goal of improving your skill in listening?

◆ *See the reason to change.* You need motivation to improve—you must link your behavior or need to improve to consequences and clearly appreciate how improving in a particular area would make you more effective in your overall performance. So, you ask yourself, what's this deficit costing me, and am I really committed to changing and improving in this area? If your honest answer is "I don't care," or "I'm not sure," then don't bother—you will only be going through the motions.

◆ *Seek experiences that demand and test your skill.* Assuming you've contemplated the change and decided it's important to you, you now need to figure out how to do it—how you're going to go about improving. What are your options? You could go to a training course in effective listening—plenty of those around. Or you could read a good book on the subject, like Eastwood Atwater's *I Hear You.*

However, the research tells us that only about 10% of development happens through courseware and readings (for more information on the evidence for effectiveness of courses, see Spencer, 2001; Morrow et al., 1997).

Well then, what about diving deeper into your feedback, and then doing a better job observing some good role models? Not to be discounted, but the research tells us you can expect about 20% gain through that approach. So what does that leave you—what is the content of the other 70%?

As other research studies have confirmed (e.g., Bray et al., 1974; Mumford et al., 2000; Lyness & Thompson, 2000; Cappelli & Hamori, 2005), the other 70% is in on-the-job experience—real-time, real challenge. Okay, you think, so I'll simply have to do a better job listening in meetings from now on. Great. Only problem is, in the meetings you typically go to, you're the leading expert in the room, and you're impatient when people are talking about things that you already know and understand. So, how can you learn there? Won't you simply become passive? Not talking isn't the same thing as listening, and you need a reason to listen.

Epiphany: You need to get involved in some sort of group task where you're *not* the expert—a situation in which the outcomes you achieve depend on listening and listening well. So, maybe the answer to your development program is simply to go and find yourself the right opportunity—say, for example, getting involved in running a task team where you need the expertise of others and can't function effectively in your role if you don't listen to them and learn from them. Yep, that's the ticket: 70% improvement, if you conform to the research findings.

But wait, you didn't get where you are by settling for 70%. You want it all. So....

◆ Hit the need with every available method. What about that course you found? Go to it! What about that book your boss gave you? Read it! How about observing those great role models? Do it! And practice it in situations that demand it. Some of these situations will come about unexpectedly; in some instances they may come as a result of hardship. Be open to those as opportunities. You can't plan for them, but since about 25% of developmental experiences are ones you stumble on, it's good to be ready by keeping your development goals in mind.

◆ Reinforce it. Reflect on what you've done, make sense of it. Keep a journal. Develop guidelines, dos and don'ts, and rules of thumb for yourself that you can use to guide your behavior so that it becomes increasingly natural to you.

If you are one of the many who are drafting and implementing annual Development Plans, you'll likely find a tool like our *FYI For Your Improvement*™ 4th Edition, FYI Online, *FYI for Teams*, *FYI for Talent Management*™, *The CAREER ARCHITECT® Development Planner*, and others to be a great starting point. Also worthwhile is chapter 21 of *The Leadership Machine* (Lombardo & Eichinger, 3rd ed., 2004), which provides a thorough examination of the method we call *Assignmentology*.

Coaching Tip

Development is one of the hardest areas to address in a feedback session because it's the one most likely to trigger defense scripts. People naturally don't want to hear that others think they're bad at things, particularly those things that are important. And of course, until someone is ready to plan for change—which is often two whole steps away from simply getting information—development planning is futile. (See Prochaska et al., 1992, for an interesting discussion of how people change, based on a study of addictive behaviors.)

Case Study Challenge

Imagine that you're a middle manager who has recently received your 360-degree feedback, gone over it with your coach, and you understand it. It makes sense, and though you honestly can't say you're thrilled to learn that people generally agree that you are a poor listener, it doesn't come as a big surprise. After all, when you reflect on it, you've heard the same thing from your daughter when she says, as she has on more than one occasion, "Can't you just listen to me without always feeling you have to give me the answer?"

So, you're ready to admit that you need to address this weakness. You can see how it is limiting your effectiveness in other areas of your job, such as problem solving, and how it might be impacting the perception that people have of you as being impatient.

- ◆ Describe what your current listening skills are likely to "look like."

- ◆ Describe what you would like them to look like.

- ◆ List some possible causes of your poor listening behavior.

- ◆ Describe a job assignment that you think would help you focus on the need to develop these skills.

- ◆ Find a course you might attend to improve in this area.

- ◆ Develop a list of books you might read.

- ◆ Identify people you know who are good at listening.

To the Coach:

What challenges would you anticipate in working with this learner?

How would you address those?

_____

_____

_____

_____

_____

_____

_____

_____

_____

Enhancement Plan

///

2. Enhancement Plan: Moving an average skill to a strength

In contrast to a Development Plan, what if your feedback tells you that you're not doing badly on a mission-critical competency, but it's clear there's room for improvement? Some findings from research and experience:

◆ There is the potential of a high payoff in terms of development in those areas where you are already average or better. That is, when others agree that you are average or acceptable but no shining star in a certain area, and you agree with them, it's going to be easier to make gains than when you're trying to elevate a weakness.

◆ When you're successful in training average performers in the real behaviors of superior performers in specific jobs, they increase skill fairly quickly, and the increase can be measured in real profit and sales increases. The payoff is typically two to three times more than selecting someone who is better in the competency to begin with (Spencer, 2001).

◆ If you are at least competent in an area, you're less likely to be as defensive about it, less likely to reject feedback on that area, and less likely to resist efforts to help you improve. The 70/20/10 approach to development we discussed in the Development Plan section is a better bet for you in these average areas than in areas of weakness. Some studies have shown that there is a greater payoff in training average performers than there is for training superior performers. And this makes sense: You don't have the obstacles to change that often come with a weakness, but you have more room to improve than someone who's stronger.

Imagine that you have always thought of yourself as an adequate problem solver—maybe not the one everybody turns to when they've got a really hairy problem to solve, but at least someone who can be counted on to contribute to finding a solution. Apparently, others agree with you: Your phone's not ringing off the hook, but no one is avoiding you either. You have decided that your organization and the quickly changing and ever-more-complex environment require you to become a better, stronger problem solver. If you had been terrible at it, there would be less hope. But, even without trying to become good, you've always been adequate. Here is an area where your odds are good. You probably have good judgment and other qualities that play into problem solving, like being analytical. So, what do you do now? For one thing, you can read a great book on problem solving and systems thinking, like Dietrich Dörner's *The Logic of Failure*. Go interview someone who is thought of as a great problem solver to find out what he does,

5

how he does it, and how he learned it. Finally, get involved in spearheading a major problem solving effort.

You might ask, why do we distinguish this type of plan under its own heading, since it seems to be only an application of the Development Plan and in all other key respects has the structure of one. The reason is simple: "development" plans, as they have been applied, have generally been thought of as a remedy for weakness, a fix for what's broken. But since we know that you'll get more bang for your buck by enhancing average performance to good performance, and in turn good to superior, the concept of *enhancement* is more than a semantic distinction.

Do you want to be good...or great? If you aspire to greatness, focus on those areas where the odds favor your turning them into a strength—the more strengths you have, the better; and weaknesses are far less likely to be converted to strengths.

Coaching Tip

The typical feedback system has traditionally focused mostly on fixing weaknesses. But weaknesses are more resistant to improvement. You're less likely to encounter resistance from a learner when you start out addressing those areas in which performance is already at least average, because there is less threat for either of you to confront.

Also, once you've gotten the planning session moving in a positive direction, and you've gotten your learner optimistically thinking about improvement, it will be easier to focus on "the bad news"—the weaknesses.

Case Study Challenge

You received the 360-degree feedback today for a manager you will be meeting with later in the week. In his job as a product line manager in a large appliance manufacturing business, he is widely perceived to be a high potential and is slated for a higher-level job in the sales organization.

According to the 360-degree feedback report, here are some of his competencies grouped by strengths, average performance, and weaknesses:

Strengths
- *Drive for* Results
- Self-Knowledge
- Standing Alone
- Learning on the Fly
- *Timely* Decision Making

Average
- Decision Quality
- Motivating Others
- Creativity
- Delegation
- Approachability

Weaknesses
- Developing Direct Reports and Others
- Patience
- Compassion
- Work/Life Balance
- Personal Disclosure

What do you think this manager should be focusing on to get the greatest immediate impact, and what might the plan look like if you follow the 70/20/10 principle?

JOBS **70** JOBS
PEOPLE **20** PEOPLE
COURSES **10** COURSES

Good to Great Plan

///

3. Good to Great Plan: Moving a strength to outstanding

You might be familiar with the concepts and findings in Jim Collins' *Good to Great*. One of the key findings—and it comes as no surprise—is that companies that made the transition from good to great performers had the most effective leaders, as well as strong succession processes.

While it is outside our focus here to summarize Collins' work, we want to chime in on leadership competencies. From the research, we know what the critical competencies are for leaders. And we also know from the research (e.g., Huselid, 1995; Becker, Huselid, & Ulrich, 2001) that there are significant organizational performance gains to be realized when HR practices are integrated around a competency model aligned to the strategic plan of the business.

With such an aligned competency model, you know what the mission-critical areas of focus are for leaders. And with the information from feedback, it's easy to tell where further opportunities for improvement lie.

The Good to Great Plan is a tweak on the Enhancement Plan: Rather than focusing on using the 70/20/10 principle of development to raise average performance to good performance, you're now looking at where you can raise good to great. It's a program of continuous improvement driven by an organizational and personal vision of excellence.

Coaching Tip

Remember, here you're dealing with someone who is, by all accounts, a high performer and in the high-potential pool.

The focus in this case will be to use the feedback as a springboard to turbocharge this person's overall performance by focusing on moving strengths to greats.

Case Study Challenge

Jody, a VP in a small service company, is on the fast track. She's young, likable, ambitious, and an avid learner. She has her sights set on nothing less than the presidency of the company.

The CEO has recently enlisted your help as an external consultant to coach Jody and help her create a challenging Development Plan for the coming year.

What you've learned from her 360-degree feedback as well as from interviews with the CEO, her peers, and her direct reports is that Jody is generally seen as well balanced and strong in just about all of the mission-critical competencies, with Learning on the Fly her highest-rated item by all groups. Within the top third of all competencies, she is perceived as less strong in the areas of Innovation Management, *Dealing with* Paradox, and Strategic Agility.

Jody is somewhat stronger (although there is still room for growth) in the following:

◆ *Dealing with* Ambiguity

◆ Creativity

◆ Developing Direct Reports and Others

◆ Patience

What is the plan for Jody?

_____

_____

_____

_____

_____

_____

_____

_____

_____

Workaround Plan

4. Workaround Plan: Using something or someone else to get the same thing done

Have you had experiences when your situation didn't afford you the time to work on a weakness—when urgent circumstances demanded adequate or better performance right now, and it was clear to you that that performance wasn't going to come directly from you?

Or perhaps, less urgently, but on a regular basis, there's an aspect of your job—let's say, developing business strategy—that you're just not particularly good at and which you know you'll never be great at. You know, as others endorse, that you can *implement* strategy with the best of them. It's just that you're not by personality or inclination a comfortable strategist, and education and experience haven't molded you into one either.

Many successful people have, at times, had to work around a weakness. They had to find other resources and ways to get done what needed to be done. You can't imagine thinking to yourself, "Hmm, this task requires skills I'm not good at, so I better implement the 70/20/10 development strategy so that I can finish this task successfully," can you? If you can, then you're not one of the successful people we're talking about.

That's not to say we're advocating your ignoring your development needs. On the contrary, we're suggesting that there are other ways of meeting the requirements, given that you work in an organization and are not alone.

Nor are we suggesting that you go to your boss at your next review and say, "Hey, boss, I know you were expecting me to have a Development Plan for you to look over, but I'm no good at this, so I'm going to simply work around the problem," then hand her a document titled "My Workaround Plan."

So, where do you start? Where successful people start: with self-knowledge. Admit what others probably also know: Here's something you're not especially good at, but it's critical to your success. What are your realistic options for meeting the need (achieving the desired outcome)?

There are four primary types of Workarounds: People, Task, Change, and Self.

People Workarounds

1. *An internal stand-in.* You know that you need to do a good job of keeping people informed on a regular basis, and you're also aware of your organization's bias for keeping communication simple and direct. In your last job, with a different organization, you were criticized more than once, and by more than one person, for being rather cryptic in your too-infrequent communications. Your current role demands regular and clearly informative written communication, both printed and e-mailed, to a widely dispersed group of people.

   When you took this new job, one of the first things you determined to do was to make sure your executive assistant had great communication skills—both in listening and in writing. As a result, people now think you're a good communicator. That's called finding an internal person as a workaround.

2. *An external stand-in.* Let's say you manage the training and development function for a well-known international company. You moved into the role (out of a job in the purchasing department) because you're known for your action orientation and your ability to organize complexity. You are also strong in other relevant skills like planning and process management, provided someone else has developed the strategy. Unfortunately, you've never been particularly adept in the area of strategic agility and also relatively untested.

   In your new role, your boss expects you not only to plan the training calendar and manage the rollout of training, but also to provide strategic direction to the business leaders on organizational learning and development needs. While you are wondering whether you need to go back to school to learn more about this, you remember a friend having recently mentioned a really great consultant she worked with who came into her company and helped her develop a three-year plan aligned with clearly articulated business needs.

   When you contract with this consultant, you'll be implementing an external person workaround. (And if you work with him/her closely enough, you just may be able to do it on your own next time—if you really want to.)

3. *A new hire.* Wouldn't it be great if everyone were just like you?

   No, it would be terrible!

   Why? Well, for one thing, because you're not perfect. Like everyone else, you're not equally good at all things. One of the things you are good at, though, is figuring out what needs to get done, then hiring people who complement your skill set—people to whom you can delegate those things you're less good at, people you can trust to get those things done and done well. That's a good part of what building a great team is all about.

You say you're great at relating well to people, empowering them, and developing them? Chances are you might not be quite as good at managing the smaller details. Is there someone on your team with skill and motivation for that? Or do you need to go outside your team to find a person like that?

Lousy at team building, great at hiring and staffing, but need to accomplish both to an equivalent level of excellence? Hire a team-building expert, and who knows—you just might learn enough from him or her to become a passable team builder yourself.

The point is, you don't need to change yourself; you just need to work around bringing this particular weakness into play. One way to do that is to hire to the particular need.

Task Workarounds

4. *Trade with a peer.* What if you're in a situation where your boss has assigned you with accountability for an outcome that requires a skill you don't have, and there's no one on your team to whom you can delegate the task because no one who reports to you has that skill either? How about a peer in your group? Might you work with someone who would trade tasks with you? Ideally, someone who might gladly enlist your help on something he's not good at but you are? This is the task-trading workaround.

5. *Share with a peer.* Rather than simply swapping tasks with a peer, you might be in a situation where it is better for you both to combine your respective tasks so that you help each other, complement each other, and each do what you are best at while realizing the synergy possible in sharing.

6. *Restructure the job.* Another approach is to sit down with your boss and work out a redesign of your job so that you are no longer responsible for a task that brings your weakness into play. For example, even though you're a technology whiz, you may not be comfortable doing public software demos. Maybe someone in the product management group or in customer service could take on that responsibility.

Change Workarounds

7. *Change jobs.* What if, in acknowledging your weaknesses, you were also firm in your view that you either didn't want to—or couldn't—do anything about them? And yet you couldn't deny the importance of those skills to success in your current job? This is a case where the best choice you could make would be to take a good look at your profile and think about what other job might be a better fit to your strengths without engaging your weaknesses. It doesn't make much sense, for example, to remain in the role of team leader if you have no

motivation for delegation or developing direct reports and if you shrink from conflict management.

8. *Change careers.* It could also happen, though, that in your consideration of your profile of strengths, development needs, and preferences, you realize that you're simply in the wrong career. Ever wonder about the apparently successful research chemist who has risen through the organization to a position of senior leadership who then decides to go teach at a college or high school? Changing careers isn't something you do lightly, and a coach needs special skills to help you with this shift.

   Both of the above change workarounds are examined from a slightly different angle in chapter 6, on Redeployment Plans.

Self Workarounds

9. *Be open, and pre-declare your weakness.* Research shows that when you admit your weaknesses, people assess you somewhat more generously. For example, if you introduce a presentation by saying, "As most of you know, formal presentations are not a strength of mine," people will be inclined to be less critical. And if you're quick to dismiss this as "merely a matter of perception," consider this: Where is the noise really located? If people didn't *perceive* you to be weak in an area, how would that influence the way they relate to you?

10. *Redefine yourself.* Learn to live without what you're not great at and can't or won't address, directing your energy and attention more wholly on the things you do well and finding opportunities to put those strengths into play more fully and often.

    A note of caution, however: It is critical that you know what your weaknesses are. It's one thing to work around them, and another to simply ignore them or underestimate their impact.

Workarounds, regardless of the particular kind, are all intended to accomplish one goal: That is, to reduce the noise while enabling you to determine the best way get the job done. Become great at what you're good at, and find ways to work around what you're not.

Coaching Tip

As a practical matter, the concept of the "Workaround" may be repellent to some managers, particularly in cultures that have embraced the single concept of everyone having a Development Plan to fix weaknesses. Workarounds in such a culture may be thought of as avoidance tactics.

In coaching situations, be sensitive to the organization's views on these things.

Case Study Challenge

Allan is a product developer at a very lean company who has been moved into the role of product manager, almost without knowing it. He's strong in the development of strategy. He's an out-of-the-box creative thinker. He's good at managing innovation. He has a great sense of humor, plenty of intellectual horsepower, and is an agile learner. Among other strengths are managerial courage, standing alone, and written communications.

He is aware, from personal reflection, that there is room for improvement in the areas of listening, delegation, career ambition, and action orientation. And feedback has also confirmed that he's merely average in those areas.

Yesterday, Allan submitted a project plan which he had labored over for several days, focusing on the smallest details because he knew how important it was to get it right. Today when he got to work, he learned that his boss wanted him to convert the plan into a P&L statement.

Since Allan was not quite sure what converting the plan into a P&L statement would involve, he decided to search an MBA Web site for help. The problem is, his boss wants a quick turnaround on this request.

Allan just called you and asked for some coaching about how to fulfill or address the request.

What sort of options can you, as Allan's coach, help him design to meet this pressing need? And what might be a longer-range plan?

_____

_____

_____

Substitution Plan

5. Substitution Plan: Using something else you're good at to get the same thing done

The Substitution Plan is similar to the Workaround Plan with one critical difference: You're substituting something you are good at, not using someone else. That is, you're using other skills *you've* got to cover for or offset a weakness. Remembering that the goal is to get the work done and reduce the noise—to neutralize the impact of the weakness— rather than working directly on the weakness, you can look at other things you may be good at that you could rely on to fill the need.

Let's say that you're simply not an effective presenter—you know it, the people nodding off in the back row know it, and the people who are rummaging through their day planners over on the left and right know it too. You could go to a presentation skills seminar, of course, where an effective presenter will list and model the seven secret techniques of effective presentation, but you have little tolerance for those "quick fix" programs that promise more than they deliver. Hey, there's a good one of those in Orlando next month!

Or you could read a book on making effective presentations, but you tried that and couldn't get yourself to pay attention (so much for the effective presentation of *written* material!).

You could sign up for Toastmasters and make a speech on the art of brewing tea…but that's not your cup of tea.

In short, it doesn't seem as though you're going to work directly on the weakness, so the traditional Development Plan is not the thing you'll turn to. And, unfortunately, you simply can't get someone else to do it for you because it's in your area of expertise and responsibility, so you can forget about the people workaround too.

But all hope is not lost. You are rightly viewed as having skills at facilitation, particularly in process checking. And people have also recognized that you have a good sense of humor. Not only that, but you do a good job of organizing information on a single page in executive summary form.

It would seem, then, that you have a few good options in livening things up:

◆ You could strategically insert humor into your presentations; for example, use a relevant cartoon to make a point, or tell a humorous anecdote that bears on the subject and captures attention.

◆ You could structure the communication as a facilitated discovery rather than a formal presentation. Or you could mix it up a bit, inserting process check questions into your presentation to break up the monotony.

◆ You could distribute the main points in advance and ask people to come prepared to discuss them; you would serve as the expert resource in the discussion.

Remembering that your goal is to achieve a desired outcome—in this hypothetical case, to communicate—there are other *ways* that are available to you which make better use of your strengths and take your weaknesses out of play. In *FYI For Your Improvement*™ 4ᵗʰ Edition, you will find several "substitute" competencies under the Unskilled definitions.

Some may ask, aren't you really just finding a way to avoid the problem? To that, we would answer that it depends on how you're defining the problem. If you define it as avoiding a weakness, then we'll answer, "Yes—but," we'll add, "you're making a mistake in the way you're defining the problem." If you define the problem as achieving a goal, a desired outcome, then we'll answer, "No, you're tackling the problem in the most efficient and effective way. You're going to your strengths to achieve the same end."

So, what's the more pressing goal? Fixing all your weaknesses or finding a better way to do a great job? That doesn't require that you eliminate every weakness—only that you neutralize the ones that are having a negative impact.

Coaching Tip

When helping someone create a Substitution Plan, much as you would when looking at a Workaround strategy, be sure to take both a near-term and long-term view (a job view and a career view).

When someone is looking at substitutions for a weakness, they should also be thinking about how they can develop that need over the longer term, guided by the perspective of what they need to become better at to achieve their career goals.

Case Study Challenge

Vera knows that she isn't good at organizing things. When leading meetings, she has loads of great ideas, but as a result of being unorganized, she often can't find all her notes, and sometimes she doesn't have a clear agenda, and occasionally she hasn't given due consideration to who needs to be involved.

Those are clearly suggestive of things at which Vera is unskilled.

What practical suggestions can you give to her to help her right away? For example, what might Vera substitute for the competency we call "Organizing" that she might be good at? How could she put these substitutes into play?

_____

_____

_____

_____

_____

_____

_____

_____

_____

_____

_____

_____

_____

_____

_____

_____

Substitution Plan

Redeployment Plan

6. Redeployment Plan: Finding a better match

Although research and experience suggest that Substitution and Workaround are frequently used approaches—at least in the near-term to meet an immediate need—by real (i.e., not hypothetical or textbook) people, there are other ways to deal with feedback.

Suppose you look at your feedback and it confirms something you've sort of known but haven't really confronted: The things you're best at—your strengths—are in areas that won't make you a star in your current role, but in those areas that are mission-critical, you are weaker. While you don't dispute this finding, this job wasn't meant solely to be a springboard for your development. You also don't think you're going to change to fit the job requirements.

Further, adopting the approach of focusing solely on strengths and ignoring your weaknesses isn't going to get you anywhere in this role, because your strengths, while admirable, are clearly not mission-critical. So, how about finding a role, a department, a culture, a job that better suits your profile?

That's what we call Redeployment. It's a valid strategy for your career path, and, more broadly, it's a reasonable and effective approach to staffing (putting the right people with the right skills in the right job—getting the right people on the bus). While it may not be the path that leads you significantly higher in your organization, it has the virtues of helping you find a place that's a better fit for you and one where you can add more value to your role. Here are some Redeployment options:

◆ *Change jobs.* What if you were to acknowledge your weaknesses but decide that you either didn't want to—or couldn't—do anything about them…but you couldn't deny the importance of those skills to success in your job?

Let's say you're a brilliant engineer who has been a solid team member on big projects, then you get promoted to a team leadership job and find that you're failing because you lack the skills to manage conflict and develop direct reports. You know that these are not only areas that are relatively hard to develop, but from reflecting on experience you realize that you don't really have an appetite for leadership. Does it make sense to find another job as an individual contributor or team member where you can continue to make a solid contribution?

◆ *Change careers.* There's always the chance, of course, that if you don't want to address a need in your job, you may not be able to simply change jobs. What if, for example, you were a terrific salesperson at your company based on your ability to analyze client data, propose solutions, and build lasting customer relations, but then suddenly your company downsized its sales organization and told you that all salespeople had to start doing their own lead generation and logging a certain number of cold calls per week.

If you felt uncomfortable about that, knowing you've never been an effective cold caller and didn't even want to be, what kind of other job might you look for within your company or elsewhere? What other career might allow you to better capitalize on your strengths without engaging your weaknesses?

Coaching Tip

You'll want to tread lightly here, because when you're talking about a change of this magnitude, you're engaging the person in more self-searching or soul-searching!

People who are ready to admit defeat in a particular job are most likely feeling vulnerable.

Case Study Challenge

When the health care consulting company that Bruce worked for was acquired by a larger training and development company, Bruce was brought in to promote the new health care practice and to serve as its primary consultant. With little administrative support (he shared an administrative assistant with another small-practice leader), he was essentially a one-man shop. From his contacts, Bruce was able to generate a number of leads for the sales organization to pursue, help them craft responses to requests for proposals, assist in closing the sale, and then serve as the primary consultant in delivering services.

Bruce was known to be a very strong presenter, with a great sense of humor and a commanding presence. He also had substantial credibility with senior leaders, both within client organizations and his own organization. Coupled with legendary managerial courage and the ability to stand alone and take the heat, he was high in the succession pool.

When a reorganization provided the need for someone to manage a large group of product managers, Bruce's boss asked him to take the job. It would mean promotion to VP level, along with substantially more salary and impressive perks, twelve direct reports, and a new set of responsibilities. Bruce, ambitious and driven, gladly accepted the job.

Before long, however, he was going down in flames. It was clear that in some new mission-critical areas like directing and motivating others, delegating, approachability, and building effective teams, he had career-threatening weaknesses.

When you were hired as Bruce's coach, you went in with the idea that Bruce was simply going through a difficult adjustment period and, as a quick learner, could pick up the skills he needed. That approach, however, hasn't worked, and you've found that Bruce is failing to adapt to the new demands.

What options might you suggest now? And, what are the implications of the various options?

_____

_____

_____

_____

_____

_____

_____

_____

_____

_____

_____

_____

_____

Capitulation Plan

7. Capitulation Plan: Prefers to keep things the way they are

Have you ever sat with someone and gone over his or her strengths and weaknesses, tried to work out a Development Plan, and the response goes something like this: "Yes, I agree that those are my strengths and weaknesses. And," pointing to a place on a chart, adding, "I don't disagree that if I don't do something to address these two areas, it's going to continue to be a problem. But I've gotta be honest, I've seen this same feedback profile now for the past six times we've done 360-degree feedback, and I'm really not interested in being better at building effective teams or being more compassionate or approachable. I've tried it and didn't get anywhere. But I like my job and don't want to move. I have strengths and weaknesses, just like anyone. But frankly, I can't think of anything I need to do to be more effective in my current role, and the truth is, I'm just not going to change."

It doesn't really matter whether you're confronting stubbornness, lack of motivation to change, or some other cause. What this person is telling you is that he has surrendered to who he is and to his limitations and that he also isn't interested in a Redeployment Plan. He's no longer looking for growth.

No less a *legitimate* response to a need than any other approach, it is, however, a more clearly career-limiting one—especially in organizations that value development and organizational learning. As long as you help this person understand the probable implications and consequences of such a response, you're doing your job. How you help the person depends on the situation he's in. If there are clear and present career ramifications, it may well involve having him talk with his boss or with an HR representative or both.

Coaching Tip

You're more likely to encounter this type of response when the person you're coaching is closing-in on the end of a career and is more or less biding time. You may also face it with someone who is truly burned out and has decided to give up.

You'll probably want to ask questions in this situation rather than give advice.

Case Study Challenge

Susan has finished reviewing her feedback and looks up at you and sighs. You ask, "What does all this add up to for you?"

Susan shrugs her shoulders and says, "Same old, same old. Who cares? It never seems to affect my performance evaluation; I'm going to get the same 3% merit…" she makes quotation marks in the air with her fingers, "increase I get every year. So, what difference does it really make if people—and I know who they are—say I'm lousy at dealing with paradox and ambiguity. I mean, who cares if I'm found wanting in the area of political savvy?"

You absorb Susan's sarcasm without betraying your thoughts, then prepare to try to be helpful. What Susan doesn't yet know is that you've been in meetings with her boss discussing some new directions for the organization. You know that her attitude isn't going to fly much longer, even if she continues to meet her business goals.

What are you going to say to Susan?

_____

_____

_____

_____

_____

_____

_____

_____

_____

_____

_____

_____

Compensation Plan

8. Compensation Plan: Decreasing the noise of an overuse

Not every opportunity to improve surfaces from a weakness. In some instances, your performance can deteriorate if a strength goes into overdrive. Have you ever seen someone so wholly customer focused that he simply abandons important policies and practices altogether and creates a culture of response by exception? Or someone whose career ambition has overwhelmed her attention to her current job? Or someone who has gone from employing humor that provides welcome comic relief to being simply irrelevant or, worse, disruptive. Have you ever worked for someone or heard of someone so results oriented that he forgets about the importance of not trampling people?

Those are cases of *overuse*, and in general it's not hard for a learner to see it and agree with it when it's pointed out in feedback. And the solution is obvious and straightforward: Ease off on the throttle.

The problem is, you just can't do that with all competencies. Try telling the guy who closes 90% of his sales opportunities to "be less results oriented. Stop being so courageous. Don't take so many risks!"

"But those are the things that have gotten me where I am today," he protests, unable to hide his incredulity. Grimacing, he continues, "You're suggesting I do *less* of the things I'm *best* at?"

Sure, you can tell someone who is high in compassion that she also needs to be firm and that too much compassion encourages people to view her as their therapist, not their boss. Or that patience is admirable, but not when people are continually missing critical deadlines. But there are times when it's fruitless to argue with success or to try to refute logic.

That's when it's time to look for other alternatives—or *compensators*—other things this person is good at that can be better engaged to temper the overused strength or reduce the noise it generates.

For example, maybe this hard-charging, risk-taking leader is considered skilled at informing but isn't using it enough during the super drive to get things done. The fix is to get the person to remember to inform everyone of what's going on and why the deadlines are important. That will lessen the noise.

Our VOICES® 2005 360-degree feedback tool provides raters with the opportunity to indicate if a competency is in overuse, and in *FYI For Your Improvement*™ 4th Edition and FYI Online, we list compensators for every overused skill. Typically, it takes from one to three compensators to balance an overused strength, that is, to reduce the noise it generates.

Let's look at another example.

George, a manager in one of your client groups, is typically thought of as a first-rate problem solver. He is known for his scrupulous attention to detail and for being a systems thinker. You can count on him to find the root causes of problems, break them down into contributing factors, and see the interrelationships among those factors. His methodological approach to problem solving is admirable.

But on George's latest 360-degree feedback report, several raters, including his boss (who is the group executive VP), agreed that he is overusing Problem Solving. Comments on the report allude to instances when he's "taken too long to come up with a solution or conclusion," and someone else suggested that, "In his zeal to understand all the factors, he sometimes makes things more complex than, as a practical matter, they really are."

It doesn't surprise you to note that his scores on *Dealing with* Ambiguity have gone down somewhat on this latest feedback. While that's an explanation, perhaps, for some of what's going on, you don't think you can help George by saying, "Well look, the reason you're taking too long to solve problems is that you're not comfortable with ambiguity. Just become better at that and you'll take less time worrying about being so thorough." It doesn't work that way.

So, you think, "Hmm, I wonder what else he might be average or good at that he could further engage to compensate for the overuse in problem solving?" Given that George is himself a very good problem solver who is glad to do some research and sees the connections, you suggest he look into compensators.

George comes to your next coaching session and notes that his ratings on Action Orientation and *Timely* Decision Making aren't among his strengths, but sees that other things he's good at—among them Motivating Others, Delegation, *Building Effective* Teams, and Self-Knowledge—could be better engaged. He works with people who are good at action orientation and good at priority setting. He could turn over the problem solving to the team and step into more of a directing role rather than feeling he has to do it all by himself.

George is even more excited to point out that not only will problems get solved more quickly, but that more problems can be dealt with simultaneously as he builds organization capability through teaching problem solving methods to others.

So, we see how a strength can kick into overuse at any time, but especially when a new situation or context calls for a strength you *don't* have. (In George's case, it was discomfort with ambiguity and slight deficits in action orientation and timely decision making that converged at an important point in time to turn a strength into an overused, somewhat paralyzing skill.)

George used a compensation approach to neutralize the effect of overusing a strength. Note that he *didn't substitute* a particular competency for problem solving—but he did better engage other things he was good at as complements to his strength and took a new approach.

Coaching Tip

When you're dealing with overused strengths, be prepared to confront some aggressive defensiveness. Remember, the person you're coaching may have gotten where he or she is in the organization based on those strengths. Work with this person to help him or her discover what has caused a given strength to kick into overdrive and develop the insight to know when to ease up and, more importantly, how to adjust.

Case Study Challenge

Jim did such a great job managing a complex outsourcing project that he was promoted into a significant leadership position: managing the entire change consulting practice. What had particularly impressed everyone were his strengths in informing, planning and organizing. With an attention to detail that set a standard for the organization and provided a model for risk assessment and contingency planning, Jim was viewed as a person without limitations.

But something has come up in his feedback this year. On Priority Setting, Directing Others, and Planning, his raters—particularly direct reports—view him as overusing those strengths.

◆ What is your approach with Jim?

◆ What do you suspect he might have weaknesses in that did not previously surface when he was an individual contributor?

◆ What competencies might he more fully engage in order to decrease the noise from the ones in overuse?

Rerailment Plan

//

9. Rerailment Plan: Getting performance back on track after a stumble

Rerailment is a special application of the Development Plan. It's more serious and takes more coaching skills than the modest coaching skills required to strengthen a weakness in a competency. That is, you've received feedback that you are in jeopardy on one or more of the 19 career stallers and/or stoppers (or derailers, from the research from CCL). You're going around a hill, the guardrail isn't adequate, the tracks are slick, and your wheels aren't securely tightened. Time to heed the warnings!

Heeding the warnings is a matter of becoming aware that you have a potential problem—let's say you are generally viewed as arrogant. To work on this problem, you must accept the legitimacy of that view (aka, "owning the need"), understand the consequences of not dealing with it, and determine that you're going to do something about it.

Why are we singling out this area of concern for a special plan? Again, we turn to the research: As noted in Lombardo and Eichinger (1989), as many as "30%–50% of high-potential managers and executives derail." People on the fast track get where they are by being highly proficient in their areas of expertise, by taking charge, solving problems, and getting results. But with that profile often come some areas of vulnerability, like excessive independence, inadequate listening, lack of patience, inflexibility. In too many cases, weaknesses align with overused strengths, and—whoops!—you're off the performance or career track.

Skilled coaching is typically required in these cases to help the derailing person increase self-awareness, neutralize the noise, and then raise the skill levels associated with the positive alternatives to the problem behavior.

In confronting stallers and stoppers, remember the 70/20/10 principle (70% on-the-job learning through activities and assignments; 20% through people and assessment; 10% through courseware and readings of things like *FYI For Your Improvement*™ 4th Edition, which provides a list of typical causes, identifies associated competency factors and clusters, and discusses remedies).

JOBS **70** JOBS

PEOPLE **20** PEOPLE

COURSES **10** COURSES

Coaching Tip

When you are addressing a staller or stopper, you may engage defense scripts in that the person is likely to be unaware of this problem. After all, wouldn't a high-achieving professional with a track record of success address a performance problem if he was aware of it? Stands to reason he would.

But, depending on the nature of the problem, you may find more or less resistance.

Consider, for instance, how arrogance might be tolerated in certain situations or organizations but not in others. It also gets called "high standards" or "intelligence" or "deeply skilled behaviors."

Also, try to determine whether there are logical connections you can make between overuse of strengths and strong stallers and stoppers. Sometimes they are simply flip sides of the same coin.

What is the relationship, for instance, between overusing the strengths (priority setting, directing others, planning) we spoke of in the preceding case study on compensators and the staller we call "overmanaging"? Is it only in its impact on others? Or on one's own career?

In *The Leadership Machine*, we talk about the challenges that you as a coach are likely to encounter when working with someone who is derailing. Primary among these is defensiveness (and you should be aware of the multiple defense scripts that people engage to shield themselves from the pain of truth). But there are big benefits, as well, in saving the derailer. Remember, these are not people who are considered dispensable; they are high achievers with a track record of success, and getting them back on track is not only cheaper than replacing them, but you're also going to find that those who have been saved become strong advocates for the development process that saved them.

Things to consider promoting to the derailer, depending on the situation, include:

◆ More accurate self-assessment to increase self-awareness (this can take time to develop).

- An understanding of the derailment process.

- Outside help.

- Redeployment (perhaps temporary).

Case Study Challenge

Mary had worked for the same boss, Bonnie, for the past nine years. As Bonnie moved up the corporate ladder, Mary moved with her. And Bonnie had always been a strong champion for and mentor to Mary. Mary had commented more than once, "She taught me everything I know."

But two months ago Bonnie decided she'd had enough of this fast-track corporate life and was ready for a change. It came as a big surprise to everyone, and to no one more than Mary. Initially, Mary assumed that she would simply be promoted into Bonnie's vacated role, but that didn't happen. The general manager for the division wanted Mary to go through some assessments and complete a 360 in order to make an informed decision to promote her.

To Mary's dismay, there was general agreement among her raters that she was in danger of derailing because she was seen as overdependent on a single advocate, and they also rated her as weak in the areas of Political Savvy and Standing Alone.

What does Mary need to focus on in a plan to bolster her credibility and keep her career at her current organization from faltering? And how can you engage Mary in developing and owning her own Rerailment Plan?

_____

_____

_____

_____

_____

_____

_____

_____

_____

PROCESS POINT

We've looked at the nine primary ways to address a need when someone agrees with the feedback that there is a need. If there is one main point to take away from that discussion, it is that there's no one best way to address every need. As illustrated below, the plan depends on the feedback, the need, the situation, the context, and the person.

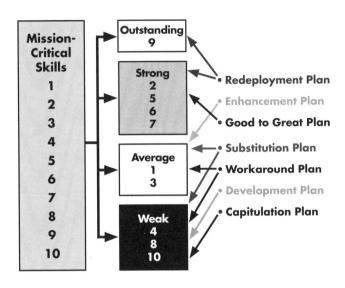

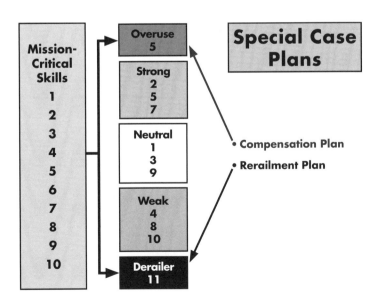

Improvement is a process, not an event. Improving performance depends first on determining where the gaps are between what is actual and what is needed. Among those gaps, you need to figure out the relative importance and potential ROI so that you can prioritize what you work on. Then decide what your plan is and what your time line is. It's a matter of determining what is doable, what is reasonable, and what is necessary. But it is not, as we have seen, always a matter of building skill, or at least not as the first step.

Typically, what happens is that you become aware through feedback of one sort or another, or through a combination of channels, that you lack a required skill in a mission-critical area. That doesn't mean that the next day you're starting to implement a plan to develop that skill, especially knowing that you're not going to get that skill immediately.

You might, as we have discussed, select one of several ways to work around the need so that you're getting the required outcomes right away.

Or, failing that—or in addition to it—you might implement a Substitution strategy. The combined goals, as we have said, are to meet the business needs while reducing the noise. Behind those approaches, though, you might have a longer-range Development Plan based on the 70/20/10 principle of development that will ultimately lead you to be skilled.

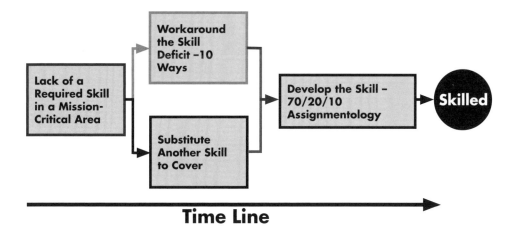

You can use a form such as the one below to capture at the highest level what approach you're going to take.

Name: _____

Skill: _____

❑ **1. Development Plan**
❑ **2. Enhancement Plan**
❑ **3. Good to Great Plan**
❑ **4. Workaround Plan**
❑ **5. Substitution Plan**
❑ **6. Redeployment Plan**
❑ **7. Capitulation Plan**
❑ **8. Compensation Plan**
❑ **9. Rerailment Plan**

Notes: _____

Date: _____ / _____ / _____

Coach: _____

In the next set of follow-up actions, we'll be looking at some other plans that do not directly involve skill building.

Marketing Plan

10. Marketing Plan: Letting others know you are skilled in an area where they don't know you are skilled

There are times when you will find yourself rejecting the perceptions of others about your skills in a critical area. Let's say, for example, that your boss thinks that delegating is a weakness for you, but your direct reports, like you, know it's a strength. This is a very simple marketing matter: Show your boss the data from your direct reports and let him/her know what you've been doing in the area of delegation.

Or, by contrast, your direct reports uniformly view you as weak on standing alone, and that's affecting their confidence in your leadership. Let them know through informational briefings what you're doing in this area, and tell them stories about the courageous stands you take on their behalf and about the projects you take on all on your own. In doing this, you'll also be modeling behaviors for your direct reports to emulate.

You might reasonably expect people who don't know whether you're skilled or unskilled in a given area to choose the rating option that is typically included in any decent 360-degree feedback assessment—for example, "don't know" or "can't rate clearly"—rather than rate it as a weakness. But even if that's the case, there is an issue for you: If what you're doing is mission-critical and you're doing it well, people ought to know about it.

Marketing, we know, is a matter of shaping perception. The primary tools for doing that are communication and demonstration. Communication, though, isn't only in what you say to people, but how you say it, especially in the particular words you use. You say you can't understand why people don't think you're strategic? Well, do you use words like "leverage" and "synergy"? Do you talk about "segmentation" and "differentiation"? While we're not advocating simply blowing smoke, it does make sense to use the language and jargon that prevail in the group you're working in, whether you like it or not.

Let people see you doing what you do. If you want people to know you have strength in problem solving, get them actively involved with you as you go through your process.

One of the additional benefits of the Marketing Plan is that while you're building your own personal brand image, you're possibly also increasing organizational learning. So, go ahead and tell your story (just make sure there's substance behind it and that you're not wasting time marketing skills in unimportant areas).

Coaching Tip

When encountering a low score (or a score lower than the person was expecting), ask where they had done this well before. It's usually in a previous job or even in another company.

Ask them to try to convince you that they are really better in this area than their score suggests. Assuming they are able to do that, suggest using that same approach and script with important people around them now.

Case Study Challenge

George has gotten a relatively low score on Strategic Agility. He is disappointed with the score. He explains that he was considered excellent at strategy in his last job at another company. He also explains that he is now so busy with his new job that he does most of his strategy work at home on the weekends. He also says that there hasn't been much opportunity to be strategic because they are just trying to put out fires at the moment.

What would you do?

What would you suggest he do?

_____

_____

_____

_____

_____

_____

_____

_____

_____

_____

Skills Transfer Plan

11. Skills Transfer Plan: Take what is working in one context and transfer it to another

Although we have waited awhile to talk about the Skills Transfer approach, it is often the place you'll want to start when confronting a need. Because it's not uncommon to find that people who aren't showing evidence of a skill in one context or setting are, in fact, relying on it strongly in a different setting.

Take, for example, Fred, who just received feedback that says he apparently lacks command skills at work, and more than one narrative comment remarks on his lack of assertiveness. Yet at the Thursday night softball league, he's the guy who's playing shortstop and also conferring with the pitcher on strategy and looking over the outfield and telling people where to play. Clearly the team captain. And when there was a questionable call one night, wasn't Fred the guy who successfully argued for a replay with the other team's captain?

So, what's happening here?

It's a matter of comfort. At the softball game, where the stakes are known and low and he knows he's got the goods, Fred is in his comfort zone and naturally takes command.

But Fred is also a perfectionist, and at work it plays out that unless he's absolutely certain about something, he's not inclined to take a public or noisy stand.

In the Skills Transfer approach, what you'll want to do is help Fred clearly see the command skills he initiates at the weekly softball game and how he can apply those at work. It's as simple as taking out a legal pad, drawing a line down the center, and on one side describing (listing) what you do to successfully display a skill in one context, then listing what that would look like at work.

When you transfer those skills, removing the attitudinal barriers to applying your skills in another context, the line you've drawn will disappear.

Coaching Tip

As a coach, when you discover a need or a weakness, before going down the development path, always ask, "Do you do this well or better anywhere else in your life or work?"

Many times people will tell you about doing it well in church, among friends, in social settings, in volunteer work, with customers, or even at home.

Case Study Challenge

Richard receives feedback that people think he is reluctant to take a leadership role on important issues in meetings. People say he holds back until there seems to be a consensus before he declares where he stands. You ask him whether he does those things anywhere else in his life. He tells you about his church work, where he is an elder and where he was in charge of last year's fund-raising efforts. He also tells you about his role on the building committee, where he convinced the other committee members to build a bigger building now with greater debt rather than waiting to build two buildings.

What would you do next?

What would you recommend Richard do?

_____

_____

_____

_____

_____

_____

_____

_____

_____

_____

Exposure Plan

12. Exposure Plan: Trying it out to see where you stand

Sometimes people will get their feedback and see a low rating and respond, "Well, of course no one thinks I'm any good at that—I don't ever get a chance to do it in my current job."

In cases like this one, it's helpful to be able to see the importance ratings, too, since if you're perceived as unskilled at something and it is relatively low on importance, addressing it probably isn't a high priority. If, however, people say it is important, and also rate you low, then you should look into doing something about it.

But what about if you simply haven't tried it, here or elsewhere? *Untested* areas are often things like negotiating or strategy that previous jobs didn't call on you to do. If it's really a matter of your not having had a chance to do it and show it, then what you'll want is an Exposure Plan. That is, you'll want to find an opportunity to put the "untested" skill into play.

Say, for instance, that people who assess you seem to think you're not good at team building. And they also think that team building is important in your organization because there's so much attention given to it in speeches by senior leaders. So, if team building is really important to your career, let's find an opportunity for you to build a team; take on a project that requires you to do that. You may *think* you're good at it; others may *suppose* that you're good at it. What we need is real data so that we can decide whether a development plan is worthwhile. So, if you get an opportunity to engage in team building and do poorly, we'll know, based on your career plans, whether that's something to start addressing.

Incidentally, if you actually *are* good at it, it's a clear bonus for both you and your organization, since it is, comparatively, a harder skill to develop and is in relatively short supply at senior leadership levels.

If you have never done this before, the most likely outcome is that you will be somewhere between average and low. Until you have had some exposure and practice, it's not likely you would start off as outstanding.

When thinking about an Exposure Plan, it's wise to *start small*. That is, you don't want to go into a high-risk situation in order to test a skill—where there's a good chance you don't really have it—if there's a lot riding on strength in that area. Or if the risk is high and you're still going to forge ahead to prove yourself, think about a contingency plan. Again, turn to *The Leadership Machine* for a broader discussion and guidance in this area.

_____

_____

_____

_____

_____

_____

_____

_____

_____

_____

_____

_____

_____

_____

_____

_____

_____

_____

_____

_____

Confidence Building Plan

13. Confidence Building Plan: Building self-esteem

Less often, you will find people who don't seem to know how good they are—or could be—at something. For example, the supervisor who doesn't know how good she is at motivating her staff. Or the office manager who really is much better at conflict management than he thinks he is. Sometimes we hear this called a "hidden strength," but, in fact, it's not really hidden—*he's* the only one who doesn't seem aware.

As you go higher up the leadership chain, you're less likely to find problems of low self-confidence; after all, it takes a good amount of it to continue to climb, whether it's a mountain or a corporate ladder.

But all organizations have some people who don't know how brightly they shine, or could shine. The challenge is to make sure they get into situations where they can get good feedback from people they respect.

In some ways this is like an Exposure Plan, except *we* already know you're good at it—now it's just a matter of helping *you* to know.

Sometimes the issue is calibration. You don't know how good or bad others are.

Sometimes it's misplaced humility—a case of not wanting to blow your own horn.

Sometimes it's a matter of a lack of good feedback.

Sometimes it's a result of being in a very talented environment of credentialed and pedigreed people and feeling like you don't measure up.

Deeper, it's sometimes the result of having parents with unreasonable standards and/or brothers and sisters who have achieved more than you have.

Coaching Tip

It's important in this plan to know why they underestimate their skills. The reason why will generally lead to what to do about it.

_____

_____

_____

_____

_____

_____

_____

_____

_____

_____

_____

_____

_____

_____

_____

_____

_____

Insight Plan

///

14. Insight Plan: Increasing self-awareness

There are times when, by contrast to a "hidden strength," you have a false sense of strength in a certain area of your performance, but everyone else is in pretty strong agreement that you're not as good as you think you are. When this situation occurs with a mission-critical skill, you're not only going to have a performance need, but a credibility issue as well.

Successful people know themselves better. They tend to agree more closely with the ratings of people who know them well. Stark disagreement usually means the person does not know himself/herself very well. This gap will lead to all kinds of performance and career trouble.

Often termed a "blind spot," it is a point of disagreement that could be mistaken for the kind of issue we saw earlier when we discussed the Exposure Plan approach. The important difference here, though, is that, in reality, you are simply wrong: The problem is not that others *think* you're weak because they *have not* seen you do this; they *know* you're weak because they *have*.

If you aren't ready to accept the feedback your raters have given, though, the way to move ahead in this situation is to get additional sources of credible feedback. For example, you could go home and during dinner say to your spouse, "You know, a curious thing happened today at work. Every one of my raters on my 360-degree feedback said I'm lousy at listening. What do you think?" To which your spouse answers, "I'll be glad to tell you, but only if you promise not to interrupt me again!" Chances are, if you ask your friends, they'll confirm it.

Self-knowledge is one of the most valuable skills you can develop, since it is foundational to so many others. When in doubt, pursue additional opportunities for insight. And remember this caution: Lack of self-awareness and insight is a ticking bomb. There are many ways in which you can learn more about yourself—many sources of feedback. Take advantage of them!

Coaching Tip

This feedback and planning event is usually filled with defensiveness, resistance, and conflict. This person believes he or she is right and everyone else is wrong.

Aside from talking about the gaps in perception, it will be a hard sell to get the person to agree to some additional assessment and calibration.

Case Study Challenge

Ed thinks he's a whiz at sizing people up. "I can tell the winners from the losers as soon as I meet them," he has bragged more than once. Based on his belief in his infallible people instincts and intuition, Ed assigns people to well-defined areas of responsibility and then closely monitors their performance.

And Ed gets pretty good confirmation of his faith in his judgment. When Ed thinks someone is a "low burner," he puts him or her in roles where he/she isn't going to be challenged. Then, when the person doesn't achieve great things, shows little motivation, and gets disgruntled, Ed says, "See, I told you."

Unfortunately, what is happening is that Ed's inordinate faith in his own judgment about people creates some bad self-fulfilling prophecies.

Ed has been a strong individual contributor and has a wealth of technical knowledge as well as other strengths his organization prizes. But in his role as a manager, unpredictable performance and higher-than-average turnover are emerging problems in Ed's group. His boss wants you to help Ed. You meet with Ed's boss, and then with Ed, as well as review feedback from his direct reports. Ed has heard it all (e.g., not empowering, overcontrolling, arrogant), but doesn't agree.

What else might you do, in a coaching relationship, to help Ed get the insight he needs in order to avoid the imminent derailment you see in his future?

_____

_____

_____

_____

_____

Diagnostic Plan

15. Diagnostic Plan: Finding out why there are large differences in perceptions

Once in a while, you will have a hard time making sense of your feedback because you're having trouble reconciling inconsistencies in ratings. You may find, for example, that your peers view you as compassionate, but your direct reports don't. Or your boss thinks you are a strong problem solver, but your peers think you have a weakness there.

More often than not, the kinds of scenarios listed above are a result of behavior on your part that is context- or situation-dependent. In fact, you may behave differently with people in the same constituency—for example, being viewed as approachable by two direct reports but not by a third.

While most of us behave consistently *across* constituencies, some of us don't. Most of us behave consistently *within* constituencies, but some of us don't.

A special case of this is a manager who plays favorites, paying warm attention to some and ignoring others.

It can also be caused by stereotyping of people of a different class or type (gender, race, religion, country of origin, etc.).

In a 360-degree feedback report, this is indicated by having a large range in your ratings (highest and lowest scores are far apart). Some say you are a 5 and others say you are a 1 or a 2.

In situations like this, the point isn't to find out specifically who said what, but to find out how you interact with various people in different situations and then to determine how to behave more consistently, particularly on the mission-critical competencies. A Diagnostic Plan would guide you toward that kind of discovery. It might involve not only your own investigation (asking people follow-up questions, for instance), but also having your coach observe you in various settings, with different people, and give you objective feedback on your interactions. You will see patterns emerge and gain insight into why you're acting as you do, and from there you can determine what you want to do about it.

Coaching Tip

As in the Confidence Building Plan, it is very important to find out the *why* behind the differences. Many times it's the *why* that points to the *what to do*.

Case Study Challenge

The people he works with, especially his peers on the leadership team, seem to think that Mark is too introverted for the hard-driving, outspoken culture he is in, and they perceive him to be weak in driving for results.

What tools are you familiar with that you could bring into play in a situation like this, which seems to call for diagnosis? How would you help Mark?

_____

_____

_____

_____

_____

_____

_____

_____

_____

_____

_____

_____

_____

_____

_____

_____

Assessment Plan

16. Assessment Plan: Finding the deeper causes of the problems

When everyone but the individual on whom you're focusing knows that in several areas he/she has glaring weaknesses and that these are causing substantial noise, you need to do something more radical. Depending on the situation and the person's openness to self-discovery and insight, this may range from approaches like enrollment in an assessment center, to assignment of a diagnostic coach, to counseling with a therapist, or referral to an EAP resource.

You're most likely to find these deficiencies in the domain of EQ (emotional quotient) and interpersonal skills or personal issues.

Sometimes it might be attributable to a drug or alcohol problem.

Sometimes it is a pending or already-happened family issue like divorce or a significant problem with a child.

It could be related to a money management issue like gambling losses or extraordinary life expenses or investment errors.

It could be an underlying health issue like late-onset diabetes or a neurological problem.

An example of this is someone who recently started having serious issues with composure and who is starting to destroy relationships at work, act inappropriately with direct reports and bosses, and is becoming a distraction to others.

Coaching Tip

Few bosses or even coaches are trained to handle and fix deeper problems like these. Each boss and coach should be aware of other more skilled resources that are available.

Think of assessment as a precursor to treatment. Make sure you know enough to refer this person to appropriate professional help.

Case Study Challenge

Shannon's performance has recently dipped noticeably. So her boss had her complete a 360-degree feedback assessment. While the ratings weren't especially insightful on most competencies, there were very low scores on Composure, Approachability, and Interpersonal Savvy.

When you discussed these results with Shannon, she seemed to you to be very closed, nervous, even mildly paranoid as she talked about how many of her peers were "out to get her."

What more do you want to probe for? What steps should you take next?

_____

_____

_____

_____

_____

_____

_____

_____

_____

_____

_____

_____

_____

_____

CONCLUSION

So that's it...for now. Sixteen ways as of today. Here is a chart showing some of the characteristics of the plans:

Plan Characteristics

Plan Type	Aware and Accept	On	Build Skill	Expertise	Probability of Success
1. Development Plan	Yes	Weakness	Yes	Moderate	Low
2. Enhancement Plan	Yes	Average	Yes	Expert	Moderate
3. Good to Great Plan	Yes	Strength	Yes	Specialized	High
4. Workaround Plan	Yes	Weakness/Average	No	Moderate	High
5. Substitution Plan	Yes	Weakness/Average	No	Moderate	Moderate
6. Redeployment Plan	Yes	Portfolio	No	Minimal	Moderate
7. Capitulation Plan	Yes	Portfolio	No	Minimal	Low
8. Compensation Plan	Yes	Overuse	Yes	Moderate	Moderate
9. Rerailment Plan	Yes	Derailer	Yes	Heavy	Low
10. Marketing Plan	Yes	Strength/Average	No	Minimal	High
11. Skills Transfer Plan	Yes	Strength/Average	No	Minimal	High
12. Exposure Plan	Maybe	Strength/Average	Maybe	Moderate	Moderate
13. Confidence Building Plan	No	Strength/Average	No	Minimal	Moderate
14. Insight Plan	No	Weakness/Average	Maybe	Moderate	Low
15. Diagnostic Plan	No	Weakness/Average	Maybe	Heavy	Low
16. Assessment Plan	No	Weakness/Average	Maybe	Heavy	Low

CONCLUSION

It's all about change. But change isn't only about fixing things. You don't need to wait until something is broken to look into how you might change it. Individual and organizational excellence and greatness are attainable—but only if you look beyond fixing what's broken to further improving what's working.

Does it matter what you call it? Only to the extent that what you name it guides how you think about it. Everything is not, strictly speaking, development. An adjustment isn't always a fix. Sometimes it's just a new way of looking at things.

At Lominger, we continue to follow the research, and when it's sufficient to justify including a seventeenth way or an eighteenth or twentieth, we'll add it to the tool kit. Not because the tool kit needs to be fixed, but because we're continuing to look at ways of change that work for people, and because our goal is to further enable you to make a positive difference for yourself, your family, your organization, and your community.

As Fritjof Capra, physicist and author, cautions: "Any isolated, or 'closed,' ... system will proceed spontaneously in the direction of ever-increasing disorder" (Capra, 1996, p. 47). When you think of addressing a need from a systems perspective, you cannot help but see the fallacy of the single approach known as the IDP (Individual Development Plan), isolated as it is from the rest of the life of an organization and the inter-relationships among all the variables that contribute to continuous learning.

REFERENCES

Atwater, Eastwood (1992). *I hear you: A listening skills handbook.* New York: Walker & Co. Publishers.

Baldwin, T.T., & Padgett, M.Y. (1993). Management development: A review and commentary. In C.L. Cooper & I.T. Robertson (Eds.), *International review of industrial and organizational psychology* (Vol. 9, pp. 35-85). Chichester, England: John Wiley & Sons, Ltd.

Becker, B., Huselid, M., & Ulrich, D. (2001*). The HR scorecard: Linking people, strategy and performance.* Boston: Harvard Business School Press.

Boyatzis, R. (1982). *The competent manager: A model for effective performance.* New York: John Wiley and Sons, Inc.

Bray, D.W., Campbell, R.J., & Grant, D.L. (1974). *Formative years in business: A long-term AT&T study of managerial lives.* New York: Wiley.

Cappelli, P., & Hamori, M. (2005, January). The new road to the top. *Harvard Business Review, 83* (1).

Capra, F. (1996). *The web of life.* New York: Anchor Books.

Collins, J. (2001). *Good to great.* New York: Harper Business.

Dörner, Dietrich (1989, English translation copyright 1996). *The logic of failure.* New York: Metropolitan Books.

Eichinger, R., Lombardo, M., & Raymond, C. (2004). *FYI for Talent Management*™. Minneapolis, MN: Lominger Limited, Inc.

Goleman, D. (1998, November/December). What makes a leader? *Harvard Business Review.*

Huselid, M. (1995). The impact of human resource management practices on turnover, productivity, and corporate financial performance. *Academy of Management Journal, 38* (3), 635-672.

Kaplan, R.E., & Kaiser, R.B. (2003). Developing versatile leadership. *MIT Sloan Management Review, 44* (4), 19-26.

Lombardo, M. (2004). *The patterns of effective managers.* Presented at the Lominger Users Conferences, Scottsdale, AZ and Chicago, IL.

Lombardo, M., & Eichinger, R. (1989). *Preventing derailment: What to do before it's too late.* Greensboro, NC: Center for Creative Leadership.

Lombardo, M., & Eichinger, R. (2006). *The CAREER ARCHITECT® Development Planner* (4th Edition). Minneapolis, MN: Lominger Limited, Inc.

Lombardo, M., & Eichinger, R. (2004). *FYI For Your Improvement™* (4th Edition). Minneapolis, MN: Lominger Limited, Inc.

Lombardo, M., & Eichinger, R. (2004). *The leadership machine* (3rd Edition). Minneapolis, MN: Lominger Limited, Inc.

Lyness, K.S., & Thompson, D.E. (2000). Climbing the corporate ladder: Do male and female executives follow the same route? *Journal of Applied Psychology, 85* (1), 86-101.

McCall, M.W., Lombardo, M., & Morrison, A. (1988). *The lessons of experience: How successful executives develop on the job.* Lexington, MA: Lexington Books.

Morrison, A., White, R., & VanVelsor, E. (1987, rev. 1992). *Breaking the glass ceiling: Can women reach the top of America's largest corporation?* Reading, MA: Addison-Wesley.

Morrow, C., Jarrett, M., & Rupinski, M. (1997). An investigation of the effect and economic utility of corporate-wide training. *Personnel Psychology, 50* (1), 91-120.

Mumford, M.D., Marks, M.A., Connelly, M.S., Zaccaro, S.J., & Reiter-Palmon, R. (2000). Development of leadership skills: Experience and timing. *The Leadership Quarterly, 11* (1), 87-114.

Prochaska, J.O., DiClemente, C.C., Norcross, J.C. (1992, September). In search of how people change. *American Psychologist, 47* (1), 1102-1114.

Raymond, C., Eichinger, R., & Lombardo, M. (2001). *FYI for Teams.* Minneapolis, MN: Lominger Limited, Inc.

Spencer, L. (2001). The economic value of emotional intelligence competencies and EIC-based HR programs. In D. Goleman & C. Cherniss (Eds.), *The emotionally intelligent workplace: How to select for, measure, and improve emotional intelligence in individuals, groups and organizations.* San Francisco: Jossey-Bass.

Zenger, J., & Folkman, J. (2002). *The extraordinary leader: Turning good managers into great leaders.* New York: McGraw-Hill.

APPENDIX

Coach/Learner Partnership Scorecard

Name of Learner_____**Date**_____

Name of Coach _____

Suggestions for use of this scorecard:

Coaches and learners should use this "scorecard" as a means of assessing the quality of their work together and as a tool to promote the kind of open dialogue that builds mutually beneficial relationships.

Circle the number on the rating scale that represents your level of agreement with each statement (1=Strongly Disagree; 2=Disagree; 3=Unsure; 4=Agree; 5=Strongly Agree).

Explore those areas where you are in disagreement on your ratings, or where you agree on a negative rating.

Coach Self-Evaluation	Area of Consideration	Learner Feedback to Coach
1 2 3 4 5	Coach was well prepared for feedback session (thorough analysis of data, causes, themes, issues)	1 2 3 4 5
1 2 3 4 5	Coach explored learner's expectations for session	1 2 3 4 5
1 2 3 4 5	Coach handled learner's concerns and personal issues	1 2 3 4 5
1 2 3 4 5	Coach probed for learner understanding and acceptance of feedback	1 2 3 4 5
1 2 3 4 5	Coach clearly explained the development process	1 2 3 4 5
1 2 3 4 5	Coach facilitated learner's understanding of alternative options/plans for addressing a need	1 2 3 4 5
1 2 3 4 5	Coach helped learner assess the benefits, implications, and consequences of various options	1 2 3 4 5
1 2 3 4 5	Coach maintained a positive, supportive style in interactions	1 2 3 4 5
1 2 3 4 5	Coach gained learner commitment to addressing needs	1 2 3 4 5
1 2 3 4 5	Coach helped learner feel more self-reliant	1 2 3 4 5
1 2 3 4 5	Coach was organizationally savvy	1 2 3 4 5

Learner Evaluation

Name of Learner_____**Date**_____

Name of Coach _____

Suggestions for use of this scorecard:

The progress a learner makes in addressing a need is premised on a willingness to be open to feedback, to understand it, to accept it, and to act on it.

Learners and coaches can use this tool as a means of assessing the learner's willingness and motivation to respond productively to feedback.

Circle the number on the rating scale that represents your level of agreement with each statement (1=Strongly Disagree; 2=Disagree; 3=Unsure; 4=Agree; 5=Strongly Agree). (Note that some of these ask you to agree with a *negative* statement.)

Explore those areas where you are in disagreement on your ratings, or where you agree on a negative rating.

Learner Self-Evaluation	Area of Consideration	Coach Evaluation of Learner
1 2 3 4 5	Learner approached the feedback with openness and willingness to understand	1 2 3 4 5
1 2 3 4 5	Learner was defensive	1 2 3 4 5
1 2 3 4 5	Learner made excuses for ratings	1 2 3 4 5
1 2 3 4 5	Learner asked questions of the coach in areas that were difficult to understand	1 2 3 4 5
1 2 3 4 5	Learner actively engaged in helping coach understand his/her expectations for the session	1 2 3 4 5
1 2 3 4 5	Learner demonstrated motivation to change	1 2 3 4 5
1 2 3 4 5	Learner maintained a positive style of interaction during the session	1 2 3 4 5
1 2 3 4 5	Learned committed to a plan of action and follow-up	1 2 3 4 5
1 2 3 4 5	Learner's plan is realistic (e.g., goals, time frames, metrics)	1 2 3 4 5

In addition to

Broadband Talent Management: Paths to Improvement

Lominger Limited, Inc. offers these products:

FYI For Your Improvement™, 4ᵗʰ Edition
LEADERSHIP ARCHITECT® Sort Cards
The CAREER ARCHITECT® Development Planner 4ᵗʰ Edition

  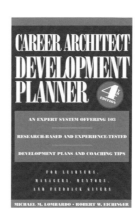

To order, visit our Web site at:

www.lominger.com